On the Path

On the Path

AFFIRMATIONS FOR ADULTS
RECOVERING FROM
CHILDHOOD SEXUAL ABUSE

Nancy W.

 HarperSanFrancisco
A Division of HarperCollins*Publishers*

ON THE PATH: *Affirmations for Adults Recovering from Childhood Sexual Abuse.* Copyright © 1991 by Nancy W. Printed in the United States of America. No part of this book may be used or reproduced in any manner whatsoever without written permission except in the case of brief quotations embodied in critical articles and reviews. For information address HarperCollins Publishers, 10 East 53rd Street, New York, NY 10022.
FIRST EDITION

Library of Congress Cataloging-in-Publication Data

W., Nancy.
  On the path : affirmations for adults recovering from childhood sexual abuse / Nancy W. — 1st ed.
    p.   cm.
Includes bibliographical references.
ISBN 0-06-250941-1
1. Adult child sexual abuse victims—Prayer-books and devotions-English.   2. Twelve-step programs—Religious aspects—Meditations.   I. Title.
BL624.5.W22   1991
362.7'6—dc20   90–55403
                                                                     CIP

91 92 93 94 95 FAIR 10 9 8 7 6 5 4 3 2 1

This edition is printed on acid-free paper that meets the American National Standard Institute Z39.48 Standard.

THIS BOOK IS DEDICATED
TO ALL SURVIVORS

With gratitude to
Susie Shinkle, a special friend and mentor, without
whose initial encouragement and faith in me,
this book would never have been begun
and to
Barbara Moulton, my editor, without whose
continued, consistent, and gentle
support and belief in me,
this book would never have been completed

C ontents

Acknowledgments

I would like to acknowledge the following people for their encouragement and support.

To Kathleen, Lalei, Robin, and Jerry for their professional and therapeutic support, and for continuing to believe that I am healable.

To Candy, Mabel, and Yvonne for their special support and belief in me during one of my hospital stays. They were my lifeline to sanity and healing.

To Diane, Greg, Judy S., Marcia, and Ruth for their inspiration, examples of courage and tenacity, and for their belief in my writing.

To Lorraine, Mollie, and David—my "old" and dear friends—for their encouragement and shared excitement in the beginning stages of this project, and for their belief in a gift I could not see.

To Angela for her continued friendship and understanding, and for always providing me with love and a vision of hope.

To Judy K., the first person *ever* to tell me I could write. I have kept this wonderful affirmation with me always and now it has come to fruition. Thank you.

To Mary and Karen, my California support network, who were among the very first to hear my first few pages and who encouraged me from the start. I will be eternally grateful for your love and your belief in me.

To Nancy H. for her support, encouragement, love, and idea of writing only fifty-two affirmations. Thanks for the permission to do what I knew I could handle and for being there from the beginning to the end of this process. Thanks for letting me just "hang around" when I needed to.

To Lisa, my wonderful sponsor and friend, who provided me with love, support, hope, and a spiritual example during one of my darkest times. I gained much from your wisdom and strength and especially from watching you walk your talk. Thank you for being my number one advocate in this process of healing from sexual abuse and for your understanding, acceptance, and respect for my process of healing.

To Claire, my first editor, critic, listener/reader of every page as it was written, and for believing in and affirming my gift. I cannot thank you enough in words for all you have done for me and given me during this process. Thanks for access to your computer when I needed it, for spending an entire Saturday with me setting up type, for loaning me your Higher Power whenever I needed it, for your honesty, for teaching me the fine art of negotiation, and for your constant belief that this book *would* be published. You are a wonderful friend and have been absolutely crucial to my healing process and the completion of this book.

To my sister, Marilyn, for believing me and encouraging me in my process of healing.

. . . and to all of the above, who listened with love and patience while I read to them my "latest" page, and who could hear in my writing something I could not. Their affirmations kept me writing and believing in myself.

Special Acknowledgments

I especially want to acknowledge and recognize the following people and places. I am grateful to you for sharing your ideas with me, which I have incorporated into my healing process and this book.

Pia Mellody for the idea of returning feelings to the offender; for the concept of spiritual, emotional, physical, intellectual, and sexual boundaries; and for the idea about how incest survivors often dress to hide the shape of their bodies.

The staff at the Meadows in Wickenburg, Arizona, where I attended treatment, for the concepts of shame, the preciousness and worthfulness of the inner child, and the idea of holding my offenders accountable.

Barbara Cherry for the idea of telling my truths and for the concept of the brokenhearted child. Thank you, Barbara, for sharing your years of experience and especially your belief in the Program as the way to heal.

Amy Fisher for the idea of surviving by "swimming for the life raft" however and whenever necessary to stay alive, and for her idea that no person is my Higher Power. You have been a very special supportive source of strength for me during my struggle with the process of healing from my incest.

Curly Munroe for what he said at a spirituality workshop about my body being the property of me and my Higher Power. I also want to acknowledge my belief that Curly truly *knows* what it means to be on a spiritual path, and he has inspired me to continue to seek my own

Introduction

It is especially difficult for those of us who survived sexual abuse as children to learn to be kind and loving to ourselves and to begin to think of ourselves as unique, lovable, and worthful people. We *are* enough just as we are. Our most important task in life is simply to *be*.

I have written this book to encourage you and me to take time to learn to love ourselves just as we are, and to learn to live beyond the limits placed on us by our abusive experiences. We have all lived alone too long with our secrets and pain. Now we can begin to share with one another and know that we never again have to "handle" a situation alone. There is help—within each one of us and in trusted people around us. We have all survived up to this point and have done it well. Now it is our turn to *live*.

I have included many topics, such as memories, fun, relationships, grief, sexuality, feelings, spirituality, body image, touch, safety, and validation. I have also referred to the "child-within" or "inner child" frequently. This concept of the "little voice" or "gut" feeling of hope inside of me has been crucial to my recovery. To remember that, as a child, I experienced so many losses, helps me to be kind to that still-developing part of myself. She was and is so precious. If another term fits better for you, I invite you to substitute it wherever and whenever you feel a need. This book began for me and is now for you as well. Please make it fit for your unique self and personal path of recovery. Use the Personal Index at the end of the book to index pages by topic as they work for you. Use the blank pages provided in the Notes section to record your thoughts and feelings. This is yet another way for you to personalize this book to fit your needs. There is also room to write your own affirmation at the end of each entry. Enjoy and be *you!*

This book is intended for all survivors of childhood sexual abuse. I have written it in the first person female because that is who I am and who I need to affirm. If you are a male survivor, please know that this book is also intended for you. For simplicity, I have referred to my abuser as male. If that fact is different for you, I invite you to change the words to suit your experience.

I have included references to a "Higher Power," a "power greater than myself," "God," and "spirituality," because that is how *I* believe I will recover from my sexual abuse. I have come to believe that childhood sexual abuse is a very intense form of spiritual abuse. When a caretaker abuses us instead of protecting us, we learn a very skewed view of the positive forces in the universe.

When a person sexually abuses a child, he is saying to that child, "I am more powerful than you. I can do anything I want to you. I am a power greater than you." I believe in order for that child to recover from this spiritual abuse, she needs to reach out for a new Higher Power—perhaps even create one. With *some* concept of a Higher Power, this child can begin to experience support and the sense of having something or someone always with her. Perhaps that power comes from within her, or perhaps it comes from other people or nature. Whatever she chooses to call that power, I believe that the recovery of the spirit is what will help her heal from her sexual abuse. My own healing in these two areas goes hand-in-hand.

I wrote this book from personal experience and need. When I began writing, there were no affirmation books for sexual abuse survivors so I was encouraged to take care of my own needs today, as an adult. So I began to write—a page at a time—taking many breaks for my own intense healing. What you will read in this book comes from my heart and my search for serenity, peace, and hope on my path to recovery. I expect my path to continue, not always in a straight line and not without bumps, detours, and stop signs. But I have an inner spark of life that requires fanning on a regular basis. In my recovery I am trying each day to honor my inner-child's need to be heard, and I believe this is the way to the serenity I have longed for.

If you are offended or disagree with the genders I have used, or with my reference to a Higher Power, God, a power greater than myself or spirituality, I support you in deleting and/or adding words that make sense to you and bring comfort. I believe that each person has his or her own unique recovery process and in this book I am simply sharing mine. I hope that you will take what you like, change what you must, and leave the rest.

Above all, I hope you will be gentle with yourself and respect the pace of your own process. You are a precious, worthful human being and deserve to believe and feel these truths about yourself. You deserve to finally have and feel joy in your own being.

Affirmations

My Body Is My Own

I learned from my abuser that my body was there for him to do with as he wished. I did not learn as a child that my body belonged to me and that it was ultimately my property and that of my Higher Power.

Today, in recovery, I can reclaim my body as my own by setting boundaries, by saying what I need, and by honoring my physical health. I can be proud and joy-filled that I have a physical body that holds my precious spirit.

Today I reclaim my body—all of it—as a gift that is mine alone. I cherish it and love it and use my adult power to keep it safe and healthy.

✓ ❖ **Today I am learning to love my body and see it as the vessel for my courageous and most precious being.**

I Am Worthful

To be worthful is to know that I am unconditionally loved and accepted in the universe just for being. I am born into this world with worth, and no one can *ever* take that away from me—although many have tried.

When I can connect with a power greater than myself or any human, I learn that I am a miracle of creation—full of worth and talents.

Because my child-self was abused, I need to affirm to myself each day that I have worth—just because I am.

"No less than the trees and the stars
I have a right to be here."
—Desiderata

✓ ❖ [Today I take time to affirm my worth in whatever creative way I choose. As I do this, I take
back my power and reclaim my natural right.

I Have a Right to Be Alive

The amount of shame I received from my abuser's act may have caused my child-mind to decide that I was so worthless that I had no right to exist; no right to be alive. Shame is a powerful feeling. When it was inflicted on me as a child by an adult's shameless act, I had no defenses to keep it out of my developing self.

Many of us may have thought about suicide many times before, during, and even after recovery has begun. I believe that the suicide gesture is about challenging our inherent right to be alive. Our abusers mentally stripped us of this right, and we need to seek and accept all the support we can while we counter this message.

❖ Today I affirm my right to be alive. I affirm my right to enjoy the beauty the world gives me. And, most of all, I affirm my right to cherish myself as a valuable and precious being—worthy of life.

I Notice and Appreciate My Perseverance

Recovery from childhood sexual abuse is a long and arduous process. There may be times when we have wanted to give up, "check out," or just go to sleep and try to forget that the abuse ever happened. These are the times when we may have felt some untapped strength within that allowed us to "hang in" and move on.

We may have wondered about the source of that strength and marveled at our ability to take "just one more step." I believe that during those many times of our need for denial, our small but growing child-within exerted her ultimate strength in calling out to us not to give up—telling us that *she* needed us to go on.

The miracle is that we have listened and that we continue to listen for that voice, which encourages us to go on no matter what. Somehow our Higher Power has given us an avenue through which we can be in touch with that voice. We have been given the gift of a spark of life that refuses to be extinguished.

❖ Today I can notice and appreciate my child's and adult's perseverance in this most painful and lengthy process of recovery. As I affirm my perseverance, I honor my child's right to live a joyous and free life.

 Love My Body

Throughout my life my body has often felt like my enemy. I may have hated how my body looked, moved, or responded. I learned to feel shame about or perhaps an inappropriate "worship" of my physical appearance.

I now know that this is because someone abused my body when I was a child. The abuse may have been physical, verbal, or both. In any case, someone else's shameful preoccupation with my physical being caused me to distrust and dislike my body.

As I continue to recover, I find ways to return the shameful feelings to my abusers and take back my natural right of having my body loved and respected. I love my body by acknowledging the wonder of all its many complex working parts that enable me to do things I love to do. I also begin to appreciate the uniqueness of all my features and love them as they have never been loved before.

✓ ❈ **Today I take time to notice how my body moves and feels and am grateful for all the wonderful things it does for me.**

I Can Have Fun

My abuse may have caused me to be a serious child—
old beyond my years. Although I may have engaged
in child's play, I could never be entirely free from
worry and anxiety. The reality of my abuse or antic-
ipated abuse was always hovering somewhere around
the perimeter of my consciousness.

I may have been shamed as I grew older for continuing to act childlike in my play. Today I know
that I had a right and a need to play like a child. Today I can allow my child-within to play with childlike feelings. I deserve to have those opportunities to
be authentic that were stolen from me through abuse
and shame.

Today, in recovery, I look for opportunities to allow myself unbridled play—full of feeling and spontaneity. I look for people who can support my need to play and who like to play too!

❖ Today I ask my child-within what she would like to do for fun and I listen and honor her requests if I can. Today I take ten minutes to engage in some play, (thus) affirming the needs of my precious child-within.

I Have a Right to Feel Safe

Growing up, I became hypervigilant so I could anticipate the abuse. As a result my child-within never learned the sensation of feeling safe and protected. When I quiet myself I can feel the pain and longing of that child, waiting to finally feel safe and protected.

I have searched for and used many things in my adult life to attempt to create that feeling of safety. Today I know that only I can provide my inner child with that feeling. I do this by listening to and honoring her feelings and by taking care of her needs as best I can.

Today I look to my Higher Power—whatever that is for me—to guide me in trusting myself to be there for my inner child. Then, in fleeting moment after fleeting moment, I begin to feel that long-yearned-for sense of safety. I am at last safely at home within myself.

❖ Today I know that I had a right to feel safe and protected as a child. I allow my child-within her grief about not getting that protection, and I guide her gently along the path of receiving that wonderful sensation of safety.

I Can Create Protection for Myself Today

When I was a defenseless child, the only protection I could create was dissociating or some other form of "leaving" the scene of the abuse—at least in my mind.

Today I recognize that I am an adult and have access to many forms of protection. All I need to do is discover and use them. At first I may need assistance in thinking of ways to create protection for myself—I am so used to being in my mode of victim thinking. As I become more familiar with my choices, I can begin to create protection for myself in scary or potentially unsafe situations.

As an adult I have the right to leave a situation I deem dangerous or threatening to me. I can call

for help whenever I feel I need it. I have *many* resources in my life today. I can refuse to engage in any
activity that does not feel safe, and I can remove myself from people who my "gut" says are unsafe. I can
do all these things using my adult thinking and judgment and without embarrassment. I do *not* have to
justify my actions. I have the right to be protected.
The more frequently I listen to my child-within's "red
flags," the more I affirm her rights as well.

❖ **Today I am willing to listen for the "danger" sig-
nals from my child-within and to use my adult
creativity to create the protection she and I
need and deserve.**

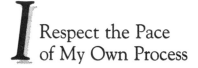

I Respect the Pace of My Own Process

Because my abuse as a child was so profound—spiritually, emotionally, and physically—I have been waiting all my life to feel good.

Abuse filled my childhood with so much unhappiness and so little respect, that I feel as though I have been waiting *forever* to feel differently. I want to feel better now; I want all that pain, anger, and fear to go away *now!*

This is when I need to be most gentle with myself. As I begin to recognize my uniqueness in the universe, I become more willing to accept the pace of my own unique process. My process is like no one else's. My recovery is like no one else's. My pace is my pace. As I begin to respect this pace, I learn to trust that I won't hurry myself to do something before I am ready.

✓ ❈ **Today I am learning to be gentle and patient with myself. As I am able to accept that my Higher Power knows what is best for me, I learn to let go and relax with my process.**

Have a Right to Tell What Happened to Me

As I was abused I learned that what happened was not OK and that, if I told, I would be not OK either. I may even have been threatened by my abuser about the consequences of telling what happened.

Perhaps no one came to help me when I was abused. Or perhaps I did try to tell people, but they either ignored me or didn't believe me. Because I was a child, I may have come to believe that telling someone or asking for help was useless and that not being believed and protected was "normal."

Today I know that I had a right as a child to tell what happened. I had a right to be protected from further abuse, and I had a right to receive nurturing and comfort after the abuse occurred.

❖ Today I nurture my child-within and listen to her feelings about being ignored and unprotected. I affirm her right to tell what happened and allow her to express her feelings about that. I hold her gently in my heart as she does this very difficult and courageous work.

I Am Patient with My Need to Trust

Trusting is probably one of the most difficult developmental tasks I have to master. As a result of my abuse, I learned that no one could be trusted—not me, not God, and certainly not other people. I may have lived most of my life in fear, yet with a longing to at last be able to relax and trust someone or something.

As a child my natural inclination to trust was stolen from me by my abusers. Even after repeated attempts at trusting others, I did not experience a feeling of safety. People in my family were loyal to the secret about the sexual abuse and could not provide a natural trusting environment for me. So, as a child, I quickly concluded that life and the world were not safe.

As I recover from my abuse, I need to be most gentle and patient with my need and *longing* to trust. I have lived my life for so long from a position of fear and distrust, that I need to be patient and slow with myself in developing this ability.

I can allow myself to take small risks in trusting as I "test the waters," and I can appreciate my valiant efforts to change.

❖ **Today I affirm my need and natural right to trust by acknowledging my longings, and by demonstrating through my behavior that I am moving in the direction of trusting at my own unique and precious pace.**

I Am Grateful for the Loving Guides That Affirmed Me as a Child

Somehow I have arrived at this spot in my life today—a place of recovery and healing. I may often wonder how, in the face of such terrifying and intense abuse, I have been able to begin to heal and recover.

The miracle of my recovery is due in part to the loving guides that my Higher Power has provided for me along my journey. Although there are times when it is hard for me to identify them or believe in them, somehow I have received from them affirmations of my worth and being that enable me to be alive and healing today.

Today I can take time to identify and appreciate the many loving guides that affirmed my worth and preciousness as a child. These guides may be people, animals, or a sense of belonging to the world through nature. Whoever or whatever these guides were, they helped to fan the flame of my life spark and allowed my spirit to stay alive.

✓ ❈ **Today I acknowledge the loving guides in my life and thank my Higher Power for putting them there.**

25

I Have a Right to Have My Requests Heard and Honored

As a result of my abuse, I learned quickly that I had no rights, especially those that centered around <u>being heard</u> and <u>recognized</u>. As a child I needed to be heard by my caregivers and I tried, often *quite* creatively, to somehow get their attention. I may have sacrificed my safety in an attempt to be heard, but those appeals fell on deaf ears. I may have surmised that I must not deserve to have my requests honored, and carried this belief into my adult relationships with myself and others.

Today I know that <u>I had every right to have my simple, childlike requests heard and honored</u>—even if it meant that my caregivers lovingly and gently said "no" to those requests. I know that I deserved to be recognized and heard simply because I existed and was a gift from God.

Today I can affirm that child's need to have her requests heard by giving them a voice through my adult-self. I can tell others what I need and know; that those requests deserve to be honored. If people choose not to hear or honor my requests, I know that their choice has nothing to do with my inherent worth or rights.

❖ **My rights need never disappear or be buried again. Today I can hold on to them and know that I deserve to have every one of them.**

Can Separate What Was
Done to Me as a Child from
Who That Child Was

Having only a child's mind, I decided that who I
was as a child was directly related to my abuse. Since
I had no one to tell me that I was precious and worthful, no matter *what* others did to me, I surmised that
what was done to me was who I was—shameful and
terrifying.

I carried these feelings into my adulthood and
continued to wonder why I had so much self-loathing
and so little self-esteem. I may have even tried to
rid myself of these "demons" by trying to do away with
myself. Perhaps I could see no other way to relieve
myself of these overwhelmingly painful feelings.

I have learned in recovery that those feelings
of shame and terror were not at all a part of who that

child was. They were feelings passed on to me by my abuser's shameful and terrorizing acts.

With my recovering adult thinking, I can separate the acts of my abuser from my precious and worthful child. I do this by affirming that child and by walking with her through the grief and process of returning the shameful feelings to her abusers. I become lighter and more joy-filled as I continue to let go of shame that does not belong to me and as I allow myself to have the feelings about what was done *to* me.

❖ **Today I can return those feelings to the rightful owners so that my precious and worthful child can at last emerge.**
(self)

I Have a Right to Have Nurturing Nonsexual Relationships with People of Both Sexes

As a survivor of sexual abuse, it may be difficult for me to trust that my relationships with others can be nonsexual. I may still retain my child's belief that people, in the end, are only attracted to me for sexual reasons.

Today I can affirm my right to have nurturing relationships with people of both sexes by taking very small risks with people I trust. I can protect myself by being clear with others about my needs and boundaries. I can ask others if they can honor and respect these needs and parameters and trust that they are telling me the truth.

I may have great pain and grief about never having received this nonsexual nurturing as a child. I can be patient and supportive of myself as I begin to experience a new kind of clean, clear, and safe relationship.

❖ Today I affirm that I am much more than a sexual being. I claim my natural right to be nurtured safely, and allow myself opportunities to receive this.

I Can Tell People How I Feel When They Act Sexual toward Me

Because of my abuse, my sexual feelings may be very confusing to me. I was taught through my abuse that sexual feelings were connected to shame. Now I may have difficulty honoring my natural sexual feelings. I may continue to hold on to the fear that I cannot talk about the sexual behavior of myself or others.

Today I know that it is OK and very appropriate to notice when I feel sexual toward someone *and* when I feel someone is acting sexual toward me. Others' sexual behavior may be communicated to me through speech, body movements, or touch.

Today I can be appropriate with my sexual feelings and expect others to be appropriate too. I can tell people how I feel when I perceive them acting sexual toward me. I may feel fear, anger, sadness, excitement, or all of these. It is important for me to tell others how I feel and set boundaries so that my child-within will feel protected. I do this by examining my motives for telling someone and then expressing my feelings and needs directly, honestly, and clearly.

❖ Today I claim the right to express my truths about sexual behavior and honor my own emerging healthy sexuality.

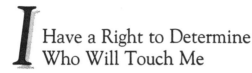 Have a Right to Determine Who Will Touch Me

I learned as a small child that I had no rights where my body was concerned. As a result I was subjected to indiscriminate touching by adults that did *not* feel good or nurturing to me. I accepted those uneasy and scary feelings as something that, as a child, I was obligated to endure.

In recovery I am learning about boundaries and realize that I have a right to determine by whom and how I will be touched. I can say "no" or "yes" to others who want to touch me, depending on how *I* feel. Today I have choices.

Today I honor the "radar" that I have had all my life that tells me—if I listen—when and with whom touching is OK. My inner voice, along with my adult observational skills, teaches me who safe people are.

As I continue each day to listen to my inner voice of truth, I learn to determine who safe people are and who I can ask to help me meet my natural needs for touching.

Just for today I will seek out a safe person and ask him or her for a hug or a pat on the back and simply notice how that feels. Today I will also remember that I always have the right to decline being touched by others, or that I can tell them *exactly* how I want to be touched.

✓ ❖ **Today I am in charge of my own physical boundaries.**

I Can Choose to Be Sexually Inactive during Times of Intense Healing for My Child-Within

My perceptions and feelings about my sexuality have probably always been skewed and confusing. As I have come to learn about my sexual abuse, the cause of some of this thinking and feeling is at last making sense to me. However, *I am the one who will need to relearn healthy attitudes and accurate information about my own sexuality.*

As I am in the midst of my healing process from my sexual abuse, I can choose, at my most vulnerable times, to be sexually inactive. This choice can provide protection and safety for my terrified child-within, who may be flooded with scary and confusing memories. Her feelings may be very intense as the memories become real to her, and my adult self will need to provide the protection and gentleness that she never received. She deserves to be gently nurtured and protected.

To be sexually inactive may create conflict for my adult if I am involved in or considering being involved in a sexually intimate relationship. Only I will be able to make the decision that is best for me, since I know my healing process intimately. The important thing is to tell my truths—to myself especially, and to others—and to be gentle and patient with my child-within. She deserves my respect.

❖ **Today I will take an honest look at and respect the needs of my child-within regarding her feelings about my adult sexual activity.**

I Deserve to Wear Clothes That Flatter the Shape of My Body

I may have grown up with the fear that if I wore clothes that revealed the shape of my body, I was "asking" to be sexually abused. Although I may, at times, have experimented with dressing to compliment my body, I could never quite feel confident that this was OK and healthy.

As I am recovering from my sexual abuse, I am learning that I no longer have to hide my body under shapeless or colorless clothing. I can release the shame about my body and know that its shape is beautiful and worthy of respect.

Today I know that the way I choose to dress is up to me and is not necessarily a reflection of my sexual intentions. I can choose garments that flatter my body and proclaim my femininity. I no longer have to fear that how I dress myself will determine the behavior of someone else. This is not possible. I affirm that I have no control over others' thoughts, feelings, or behavior.

Today I am free to dress exactly as I wish—to feel my sexuality and embrace it. If old feelings surface and make me feel unsafe with how I express myself in my dress, I can listen to those feelings and reassure myself of my rights. I need never fear that the sight of my body will bring abuse.

⟐ I use my adult recovering self to dispel those old feelings of fear and to affirm my rights and sexuality.

I Am Learning to Love and Trust the Many Responses of My Body

In the past I have felt so confused and betrayed by my body's responses that it has been difficult for me to learn to trust my body. I now know that my child-body was taught many "miscues" by my abuser. Feelings that are naturally pleasing became fear-filled and linked to pain. My young mind was conditioned to mistrust the natural responses of my body.

I am slowly learning in recovery simply to notice my body's responses without judgment. This is difficult, but it is the beginning of "reprogramming" my mind and body to a natural way of responding.

Because my body was so abused, its network of responses is very confused and cross-wired. Each time I notice a response to some stimuli and simply accept it, I am moving toward a love and trust of my body.

❖ Today I affirm my right to reclaim all of my body's responses. I hold them to my heart as unique and special parts of me.

I Can Reach Out for and Accept Help

Throughout my process of recovery, I may experience periods of time when I feel hopeless and overwhelmed. It is during these times that I need to reach out for and accept any help that I can get. I may not always like the form the help takes, but if it helps me stay alive and is not self-injurious, then I need to accept it as a natural part of my process.

There may be many times when I would rather give up than have to once again accept help. Each time that I go on, despite my misgivings and strong doubts, I am honoring and affirming my right to live a joyous and free life.

When I am feeling overwhelmed and frightened, I will look for the help that my Higher Power is providing for me and will accept it with as much gratitude as I can. I will continue to look for God's purpose in all that is presented to me and affirm that, at all times, God is working for my greatest good.

❖ Today I affirm my right and ability to reach out for and accept all the assistance my Higher Power is offering to me along my journey.

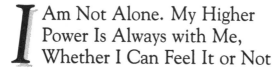# I Am Not Alone. My Higher Power Is Always with Me, Whether I Can Feel It or Not

When I experience times of feeling utterly alone, I can remind myself that my Higher Power is with me and knows how I feel. This concept may be difficult to trust, but if I continue to affirm this, I will come to believe it.

My abuse experience taught me that I was all alone and that there would be no help or support forthcoming. I internalized that feeling of total aloneness and may continue to carry it with me on a daily basis. This is where my hopelessness lives and flourishes.

Today I need to affirm that I am no longer a helpless and frightened child. I am an adult who has many choices. One of those choices is to reach out to others and tell them how I feel. I can help my child-within feel her feelings about having been left so alone and helpless, and use my adult-self to reassure her of protection.

My child-within may have some difficulty believing in a Higher Power because she may not yet have experienced someone "coming through" for her. As I am able to be there for her and allow others to be there for her too, I nurture her inherent need to believe in a protective and loving spiritual being.

❖ **Today I remember that I am not alone.**

I Am Learning to Trust My Memories

Memories seem to lie somewhere between day-to-day reality and our nighttime dreamworld. Memories are often ephemeral and leave a large margin for questionability. As I begin to have memories about my sexual abuse, it will be normal for me to wonder if they are emanating from my nighttime dreamworld or from an actual occurrence in my life. I may even question them by noting my "vivid imagination."

It is normal for our memories to feel unstable and questionable. After all, many of them *were* mixed in with our nighttime dreamworld if we were sexually abused in our beds at night.

As I learn to trust my memories as data that I need for my healing, they will seem less like my enemies. No matter from where the memory emanates, it is mine and it has a message for me.

I probably have been told that many things that I said or heard as a child were not real. I may even have even been told that I was crazy or must have "imagined" those events.

Today I take back the power of my own mind by respecting the data it is providing for me through my memories. My memories do not have to be logical or "make sense." My memories are my friends and will lead me down the path of healing and wellness.

❖ **This day I am learning to trust and accept my memories.**

My Anger Can Provide Strength for Me to Deal with My Memories

Anger may be a feeling I have learned to repress or abuse. I need to believe that my anger, like all of my feelings, is OK and a necessary part of being human.

Because it was not safe to be angry with my abuser, I may have internalized my anger until it became self-loathing. In recovery I need to seek assistance in separating my inner-directed anger from my everyday errors. As I focus on the appropriate recipient of my anger—the abuser—my self-loathing begins to dissipate and my self-love grows.

I can learn to use my anger as a source of strength to deal with the memories of my abusers as they surface in my consciousness. I recognize my anger and affirm it. I use my adult anger toward my abuser as a means of demonstrating to my child-within that I will continue to hold our abuser accountable. As I do this she can see that *her* anger is valid and that she is extremely worthful.

✦ **This day I accept that my anger can provide me with strength.**

I Am Slowly Coming to Believe That There Is, and Always Has Been, a Power Greater Than Myself at Work in My Life

If I look back at all the events in my life—both positive and negative—I can see that there was always another hand at work in them. When I felt that my world would end, it didn't. When I felt that I had no more strength or will left, I did. When I felt that there was no one there, someone appeared.

I am coming to believe that, in reality, I had no control over these happenings; that there was a force greater than myself at work in my life. I can still refer to these workings as "coincidence," but that does not change the fact that I had no control over the outcomes.

As I grow in recovery, I become more willing to believe that there is, after all, a Higher Power at work in the universe. My child-within may need to express her feelings about this directly to that Power, since she has felt so alone and unsupported. I can even allow her to be angry with this Higher Power. This is how she will receive healing and learn to trust.

❖ Today I affirm that I can take my time with my belief and trust in a Higher Power. My Higher Power understands my need to go slow and will support me in my process.

I Am Perfect Just as I Am

To affirm that I am perfect just as I am does not mean that I am flawless. It means that I am at a place of accepting myself right where I am. I am not expecting myself to be somewhere or someone else. I am exactly where I am supposed to be.

As I affirm this perfection, I am accepting all of me — my strengths, my weaknesses, my dreams, my secrets, and my past. I am all of these things and I am learning to love me.

Today I accept my past and my present and cherish all the events that have made me *me*. Even the most negative experiences have given me gifts. My sexual abuse has given me the gifts of compassion, perseverance, courage, and wisdom. I am *not* saying that I am grateful for the abuse. I am saying that today I can recognize and cherish the parts of me that have kept me alive and given me a passion to live.

 Today I am perfect—because I am accepting *me*!

Today I Take Time to Notice the Beauty of the World

Often I get lost in my own internal chaos of reliving the past and weighing the future. These are the times when it is most important that I take a deep breath and reconnect with the many things in this world that support my spirit.

Wherever my eye rests today, I see beauty. As I go through my day, I notice my surroundings and find beauty in all I see. I may see, feel, smell, and hear the beauty. The world offers me an endless variety of wonder and loveliness. Today I use all of my senses to experience the world I am in.

I may notice the flight of a bird as it soars on its life's journey, or the sight of the light on the water as it creates a rainbow or sparkle that only it can create. Perhaps I hear something in nature that calls to my life spark, or in another person as she shares a part of herself with me.

 Today I take time to quiet myself and notice the wonders of the world in which I live.

I Can Allow My Child-Within as Much Time as She Needs

As a child I was hurried to do things before I was ready. Someone else's needs always came first, and I learned to relegate my needs to a position of lesser importance. I may have come to believe that my needs weren't important. Others' timing became my timing.

As I recover from my abuse, I learn that I must come first. I talk to my child-within about her needs on a daily basis and allow her all the time she needs to do something. This will become a constant permission-giving process as I affirm my child's needs as coming first. Whatever she needs to do, say, or feel, I allow her the time she requires.

I affirm that I have all the time in the world for her each time I give her internal permission to have her needs met. I no longer allow others' expectations or timetables to become mine. I honor and respect my own unique timing and allow my precious child all the time she needs. She has waited so long— she deserves to finally go at her own pace.

 Today I take my time.

I Have a Right to Grieve My Losses

When I was sexually abused, I experienced a deep sense of loss: loss of dignity, loss of power, loss of control, and even a loss of self. In order to survive these losses, I created a special place in my mind for these memories. The memories remained there until I was ready to remember and deal with them. My mind and body have a wonderful sense of timing and will not betray me.

Today I know that in order to fully heal from the losses caused by the abuse, I must begin, little by little, to have my feelings about the memories. Grieving is a natural process for moving through these feelings. I have felt the denial for years. Now, at my own unique pace, I begin to feel the anger, the bargaining, then the intense pain and sadness, and finally, the acceptance and resolution.

My grieving will take as long as I need it to take and I have a right to all the time I need.

❖ Today I give myself permission to fully grieve my losses at my own gentle pace.

I Can Allow Myself to Be Supported as I Grieve

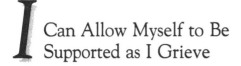

I have spent so many years keeping the secret of the abuse from others and perhaps even from myself, that it may be difficult as I begin to grieve to allow others in as support. This secret is one I have borne so long, alone and ashamedly, that I may have come to believe that no one would believe me, much less support me in my process of healing.

As I recover I learn that my grieving process is a necessary means for me to "walk through" these painful memories. Today I believe that I have a right and a need to be supported by others during this process. I am reexperiencing some intense losses that I have held to myself for years.

Today I allow myself to be supported in any way that feels safe to me. Other people can be there for me to lean on now. I can finally let down my guard and express the feelings I have held onto for so long.

❖ Today I allow other people to support me as I grieve. This is a gift that I give to myself.

I Was Born Precious and Worthful

In recovery I begin to notice the absolute and undebatable preciousness of babies. Whenever I see a baby, I see the preciousness and worth that our Higher Power grants to each soul born into this world.

If I can look at a baby and realize that I was once that young, I can also believe that I too was born precious and worthful.

I may experience deep pain as I come to this realization. This is part of the grieving that I need to do for my child-within. My preciousness and worth may never have been "seen," or perhaps these qualities were stripped from my consciousness a little each time I was abused.

Today I imagine myself as a precious and worthful newborn and I slowly and gently bring these qualities into my adult-being. These qualities were never lost to me. They were simply buried beneath layers of shame and guilt—the shame and guilt of my offender.

❖ **Today I begin to see myself as a precious and worthful person and affirm this in any way that I choose.**

I Deserve to Have Dreams

I learned through my abuse that dreams and wishes did not come true and that it was fruitless to bother thinking about them. I saw how my wishing did *not* stop the sexual abuse. Still, I escaped the reality of the abuse through dreams that never came true.

Today I can thank my child-within for her creativeness in dreaming to survive the abuse she suffered. Dreaming was her way of staying out of reality when life became too painful and terrifying.

In recovery I am learning about my need and *right* to have dreams, whether they come true or not. My dreams and wishes sustain my need to look beyond my present-day existence and keep me growing along spiritual lines; for in dreams there is hope.

If I can see each of my dreams as a gift from my Higher Power, I will be able to allow the outcome to be further lessons for me about my life and journey.

 Today I embrace my dreams, knowing that I deserve to have every one of them.

I Am Courageous

If I have ever doubted my courage, I need only observe that I am alive. To have survived the atrocities and often violent abuses that were inflicted on me as a child, I needed and possessed a tremendous amount of courage.

Today I may not always see my own courage, but I can be reminded of it by others to whom it is so clearly apparent. I can allow people I trust to mirror times when they see me acting courageously— and begin to believe it myself.

I have gone through extremely painful times in my life, when I thought I would never emerge once again into the light. It was during these seemingly hopeless times that I was most courageous. To feel the intense fear, loneliness, and pain, and still go on, is perhaps the most courageous act of all.

❖ This day I accept that I am indeed a most courageous person.

I Have a Right to Hold My Abuser Accountable for His Offensive Behavior

When I am feeling self-loathing or hopelessness, let me ask myself with whom I am angry. Chances are that the real focus of my anger is my abuser. When I was a child it was most unsafe for me to be angry with the powerful offender. So, instead, I turned the anger inward. This is the way my creative child survived the terrifying and horrendous abuse.

Today, in recovery, I remind myself that I am an adult and can support that frightened child-within with my adult anger. I recognize and affirm my right to hold my abuser accountable for his offensive behavior toward my child-self. I do this by acknowledging what happened and by directing my anger and other negative feelings toward the appropriate person: the offender.

No longer do I have to protect myself by shielding the offender from the consequences of his behavior. I am free today to have all my feelings about the abuse, then let go and go on with my life. I do not blame the offender, because that keeps me emotionally tied to him. Rather, I tell what happened, how I feel, and send the responsibility for the offensive act back to the offender. Then, and only then, will I be free.

❖ Today I give myself permission to hold my abuser accountable.

I Can Create My Own Higher Power

Being raised in an abusive family, I learned that my first "higher power"—my parents—was not protective, loved me conditionally, and would punish or leave me if I made a mistake. I could only visualize a punitive higher power. This belief may have created a lot of confusion and hopelessness for me as a child. I believed that no one would ever truly be there for me.

As I mature in my spirituality, I can begin to think about and create my own personal Higher Power. I can create this entity in my own mind and soul and give it all the attributes that I needed and *deserved* in my parents. I can begin to believe that I deserve to be alive on this planet and that there is some loving force that will support my choices for *life*.

✤ Today I can begin to think about and create a positive, nurturing Higher Power of my own choosing.

I Honor My Child's Courage to Survive

When I think back on all the travails and odds that my child fought against—just to survive—I marvel at her courage. I am amazed that such a small spirit could prevail in the face of her many abuses—some on a daily basis.

I can learn to appreciate this young child's courage today by observing other survivors of sexual abuse rail and fight against the offender feeling—shame—that tells them that they do not deserve to live.

Each time I see a survivor turn toward life by confronting the sometimes all-consuming feelings of shame and fear, I can celebrate my own child's miraculous courage to survive. She truly has been a warrior *and* a gentle soul, waiting to be loved and recognized.

Today I express my gratitude to my child-within for her valiant and persistent efforts to survive while all else was telling her to die.

❖ Today I celebrate my child-within's life by daily removing offender thoughts of shame and fear from *my* thinking.

I Am Creative

I may often look at other people and marvel at—
perhaps even envy—their creativity. I can readily see
and appreciate the life force within these "chosen"
human beings that allows them to express themselves
creatively and share their gifts with others.

If I am only seeing creativity in certain people,
I am surely missing the creative spirit that resides in
everyone—including myself. I have only to notice
how creative I was as a child in surviving and even
flourishing during extremely frightening experiences.
Somehow that small spirit created thoughts and fan-
tasies that allowed her to stay alive and to reach for
healing.

Today I can take time to notice my creativity as it was expressed through my child, and to be grateful to her for that gift. I can also begin to look within my adult self to see how I express my creativity today. What I envy in others is surely within myself—perhaps just in another form.

✓ ❖ **Today I allow myself to be aware of my creative spirit and how it is expressed in my everyday life.**

I Am Learning to Love My Child-Within

There may have been times in my adult life when I've wished that my child-within would be quiet or even disappear. She carries so much pain that I would rather ignore her than face the inevitable truths about my abuse. It's relatively easy to love the small child-within who represents joy and life. It is much more difficult to love the brokenhearted child-within, because she is a reminder of my pain. Yet it is this child who most needs me to see her and believe in her. She needs all the comforting and love that I can give her. She, especially, needs to know that I accept her just as she is—brokenness and all.

I can learn to love this child by honoring her feelings, her thoughts, and her creativity. She was the

one who believed in life enough to keep on going
when all else told her to give up and die. She deserves
to be heard and loved by me *and* others.

❈ **Today I gently turn my attention to my child-
within by listening for her truths and affirming
her creative survivor skills.**

 Can Celebrate the Beauty of the Child That I Was

I was born a beautiful, worthful child of God. I came into this world with dignity, preciousness, and beauty. During my sexual abuse this beauty seemed to disappear. In actuality the shame of the abusive actions began to cover up a little piece of that inner beauty until it did feel as if it were all gone.

Today I can recognize the beauty of the child that I was by looking at pictures of myself at various ages and seeing the beauty in each of those children. I can also remember the joyful and happy moments I experienced as a child. Those memories are what kept my inner spirit alive.

My physical, outer beauty may have been severely criticized, and so I may need to work hard at recognizing the beauty of each of my child's features. She always had them. She just learned from her abusers to discount them or to see them in a skewed, dishonest manner.

I can appreciate the true beauty of the child that I was each day by simply affirming *my* truths about my physical, emotional, spiritual, and intellectual facets.

❖ **Today I am willing to look for and affirm the inner and outer beauty in the child that I still carry within me.**

I Honor and Respect the Survivor Behaviors That I Created as a Child

As a child I created and used a vast repertoire of behaviors to survive my abuse. I may have dissociated, lived in a pretend world, occupied my mind with triviality, developed other personalities, and most probably buried any "unacceptable" feelings by being withdrawn, rageful, or preoccupied. These are all behaviors *and* thinking patterns that the creative, life-spark child-within created so that my spirit could somehow survive, and so that I could maintain a semblance of sanity as I withstood the sexual abuse.

Today these same behaviors that allowed me to survive and grow to where I am today may be preventing further healing. I will need to give up some of them, very slowly and gently, in my own time, so that I can continue to recover from the effects of the sexual abuse on my life. I can get suggestions and help from others, but the true changing will need to occur within me. All I need for this to happen is willingness, patience, and a small measure of faith.

I believe that in order to let go of the old survivor behaviors that are hindering me today, I need to acknowledge them and thank my child-within for her resourcefulness and creativity. She was and is a fighter who refuses to go down, even in the most adverse situations. Her life spark calls out to be acknowledged and honored. I truly marvel at the determination and strength held in so small a being. She is a real trooper.

❖ Today I spend a moment truly honoring the creative child that I was and feel grateful that she was born.

I Am Learning to Trust and Respect the Messages I Receive from My Child-Within

So many times in my life I have either ignored or discounted the messages my child-within has attempted to give me. She can be a very accurate barometer of what is safe and healthy for me—if I will allow myself to listen to her. A queasy feeling in my stomach or a consistent message of alertness can clue me in to an unsafe person or situation. Her feelings are pure and can be trusted.

I have probably spent most of my life ignoring her messages so that I could survive. I learned to "get into my head" to try to figure out things. After all of my thinking, I may have surmised that I was crazy, to blame, at fault, or wrong—but, naggingly, I "felt" differently. The feeling I was having was my child-within's attempt to let me know the truth.

Today when I find myself defending my feelings, I can almost be positive that I am ignoring the wisdom of my child-within and reverting back to one of my old survivor tactics—rationalization. This is when I can stop, breathe deeply, and practice getting in touch with my child-within's message for me. Little by little, I can learn to trust her truths and will no longer have to intellectualize to hide my feelings. I can simply begin to trust my feelings and, therefore, my *self*. This is how I will grow to trust my most precious being.

❖ **I am slowly learning to trust the truths of my child-within.**

I Have a Right to Feel Angry

As a child I may have witnessed violent anger in the form of rage—acted out or silent—and so concluded that anger was not an emotion that was safe to feel. I particularly felt the offender's anger intensely each time I was sexually abused. I may not have been aware of the anger, but it was there—many times unspoken. As a defenseless child, I was certainly unable to be aware of my own anger at what was happening to me. I was too encased in terror and was attempting to move out of the abuse experience—at least on the emotional and the intellectual levels.

Today I may still experience guilt, fear, or an entire range of other emotions *and* thoughts whenever I feel anger at some person or situation. Anger may still be a very unwelcome and uncomfortable feeling for me, and I may go to great lengths to avoid it— particularly in regard to relationships with others.

Now that I am an adult, I have the ability and freedom to learn that anger just is, and that I have a right to feel it and express it in ways that are safe for me. Today I can get help in learning to express my anger so that it can eventually feel like a normal, acceptable emotion. This may not be a simple task, and I may need to exercise great patience with myself as I learn to do this.

As I recover I will learn that my child-within has an enormous reservoir of anger and rage that she feels toward her offender. She will need a great deal of assistance from me in helping her to express this feeling in safe ways. She certainly has *every* right to feel anger about her sexual offenses, and I can assist her healing by affirming this for her. She now can begin to feel the righteous anger she was entitled to feel during and after the abuse occurred. She needs to know that she has the *right* to feel angry and that she is not bad because she feels this. She is finally getting the opportunity to feel her natural feelings.

❖ Today I affirm both my adult and child-within for any anger they feel and celebrate this with them.

I No Longer Have to Bear Unbearable Situations

As a child my choices were very limited. I could not choose my parents, my environment, or what happened in that environment. Not only was I powerless, I was helpless as well. By surviving my sexual abuse, I learned to bear situations that were terrifying and abusive to my spirit, emotions, and body. I may have dissociated in order to "stand" this abuse, or I may have buried the memories and accompanying feelings. I learned to bear the truly unbearable. It was my ticket to surviving and keeping myself and my life spark alive.

Today I am an adult and may forget that I no longer have to bear unbearable situations. I may not even recognize abusive or unhealthy situations until someone gently brings my attention to them. I am so used to numbing out, or believing that I should be "tough," that I may stay in unhealthy situations long after I need to. I can help my healing process by checking in with my child-within to see if she is feeling as if she is being asked to "bear up" once again. I can then use that data along with my adult judgment to decide if I need to leave a situation or stay. I can make wiser decisions today about what is challenging and what is hurtful if I am willing to tune in to my child-within's feelings and exercise my mature thinking.

Making changes will be a process of trial and error and so will certainly involve risk and some iota of faith. I will allow myself to make mistakes and know that I will grow from this process. Sometimes the amount of pain I am in will help me to determine more readily what I need to do to take care of myself today.

❖ Today I affirm that I can leave unbearable, abusive, and unhealthy situations. I can listen to my feelings, use my thinking, and take a leap of faith. This is how I will heal.

However I Feel about My Offender at This Moment Is OK and Valid

My feelings about my offender may vary from day to day or even from moment to moment. Particularly if my sexual offender was a parent, I may have many conflicting feelings. I may spend a great deal of time trying to figure out how I "should" feel. Instead I can let go and allow whatever feelings I am having about my offender to be OK and valid for any given moment. If my offender was a parent, I may sometimes have very positive feelings for him and even gratitude for the gifts he passed on to me.

Certain smells or the sight of objects or pictures may remind me of nurturing gifts that that person

was able to share with me when he wasn't acting out
in his sickness. I may also, at the next moment or
at some other time, be reminded of the atrocities of
the sexual acts he committed against me as a child
and feel hateful, vengeful, and disgusted. These feelings are valid as well. I do not have to discard any positive feeling I may have toward my offender simply
because I also feel very negative feelings about his sexual abuse of me.

As I begin to heal, I will be able to have and validate *all* my feelings about my offender. The important thing is to allow my child-within to have all her

feelings so she can begin to feel whole. I can help her heal, as an adult, by validating her feelings and helping her to do whatever she needs to do—safely —to express these feelings. She and I can learn that both negative and positive feelings about a person or situation can coexist and we will be OK, and very sane.

❖ Today, at any given moment, I validate and accept any feelings I may have toward my offender. As I do this I am helping my child-within to heal and become whole.

I Deserved to Have Loving and Nurturing Caregivers

We are all born into this world precious, helpless, and deserving of loving and positive nurturing from our caregivers. We are gifts to be cherished and deserving recipients of all the caring and love that will enable us to thrive as healthy human beings. When, instead, we are sexually abused by those trusted caregivers, we learn that people are there to hurt us and that we are at the mercy of these "big people."

I may have received smatterings of love and nurturing, but what I received was tainted by the abuse. I received confusing messages about my worth and my place in this world.

Today I need to grieve the nonexistence of my fantasy mother and father. As a child I needed to hold on tightly to the images of loving, caring parents. This is how I survived. Today, to accept reality and heal my authentic self, I must gradually come to grips with the fact that I did not receive the unconditional love, nurturing, and protection that every precious child deserves.

Today I must begin to see my parents as real people and grieve the loss of my "fantasy" parents. This can be a long and painful process; yet if I don't experience it, I rob myself of needed healing. I can learn and appreciate that I survived despite the lack of a basic necessity of life. This means I get to have all my feelings about this loss and also know that, as I move through the process, I am getting on with my own real life.

❖ **Today I take a small step toward acceptance of my caregivers as they really were and are. This is a gift of healing to myself.**

I Can Survive the Healing Process

I never learned that "healing" meant pain. I always saw healing as a benign and relieving process. Today, as an adult, if I consider a physical wound, I know that it will hurt initially and sometimes for quite a while as new body tissues are forming to heal that wound. So it is with my sexual abuse healing process. As I become more and more aware of the wounds through my memories, I begin to feel the intense pain that has been frozen—sometimes for years. To feel this pain is a natural part of the healing process, and I can get support as this pain occurs.

There will probably be many times when I believe I cannot survive the pain of the healing process—that the wounds are too deep. If I can but cling to the belief that I can and *will* survive this process, I can walk through any pain I might encounter. Sometimes I may need to believe I will survive because someone else tells me I can, or because I witness another survivor healing and surviving— no matter what. This is how, very gradually, I will come to a place of *knowing* in myself that I will survive.

This often-quoted phrase is appropriate as I work through my healing process: "Living well is the best revenge." If I learn to choose life—my life—and build health into all parts of it, I will be healing my wounds and "beating" the death wish of my perpetrator. I do not and will not die for anyone. I will do whatever it takes to heal. I am not on a schedule. I will heal in exactly the way and in the amount of time I need and deserve.

❖ Today I affirm that pain is a natural part of healing, and I know that I will not die from feeling it. I will survive and live well.

I Always Will Have More Strength Than I Believe I Have

I may have heard many people tell me how strong I was—perhaps even during times when I felt weakest. They were seeing in me something that it is difficult for me to claim or even be aware of. I learned as a survivor of sexual abuse that *I* was weaker—especially weaker than the person who abused me. My real gift of strength was thus "stolen" from me and has remained hidden deep within me for many years. This source of strength has carried me through many horrible and perhaps life-threatening situations. *This* is what other people have seen.

Like the grass that persists on growing through the cracks in the sidewalk, or the edelweiss flower that grows in the most adverse conditions high atop the mountains, I too have continued to push on through my own adverse conditions and continued to grow.

Once again it is that spirit within that has refused to give up, no matter what conditions I am placed under. It would not die during the abuse, and it even more vehemently refuses to die today. As I continue to choose the path of healing, I can have faith that that source of strength will continue to be there for me even under the most adverse conditions. I am strong.

❖ Today I notice my inner strength—even if I cannot feel it. I acknowledge and am grateful for that source of strength.

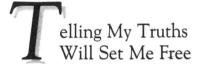elling My Truths Will Set Me Free

As I begin to tell the truths about my sexual abuse, I will notice that the voice of my offender inside me will often get louder and more convincing. The offender's voice will tell me that I am imagining the abuse, that *he* would never do such a thing, and even that I am crazy. If I listen to and believe this voice, I cannot heal. It isn't until I begin to listen to the small but wise and truthful voice of that small child-within that I can begin to heal. It is when I listen to her and believe her no matter *what* she is telling me, that she can begin to trust my growing adult. As I listen to and tell my truths, I begin to be set free from the bondage of the lies that I have believed for so long—the lies that may have almost cost me my life, my sanity, and my self.

I can begin by telling my truths—as I begin to know them—to safe people who will believe me, affirm me, and not pity me. As I gain strength I will *know* when I feel safe in telling other people that I may not know so well. This is how I will connect with and get support from other survivors.

❖ **Today I take a moment to reflect on a truth and thank my child-within for her wisdom and courage in telling me.**

I Affirm My Child-Within and Take Back My Power by Taking Responsibility for My Own Life

As a victim of childhood sexual abuse, I may have spent most of my life waiting for someone to finally come and rescue me. This childlike thinking may have kept me locked in a mode of refusing to learn to take responsibility for my own life. I may have assumed surface responsibilities like having a job, supporting myself financially, maybe even thriving in this area. To all outsiders I may have appeared to be in perfect control of my destiny.

In reality I have a small child-within still waiting for someone to finally take care of her unmet emotional needs. Part of growing up and healing is realizing that no one is going to do that for me. It is no one's job but my own now. Once it belonged to my caregivers, but today I am an adult and I am the only one who can help to meet the emotional needs of that child-within. She deserves to be attended to.

I will find that as I am willing to take even small responsibilities for my life as an adult, I begin to take back my power. I have been waiting for someone else to supply that power for me and have cheated myself out of that opportunity for growth and strength.

Today I recognize that I must continue to take back my own power from the offender who originally stole it and left me a victim. I will allow that offender to have less and less of my power as I grow into taking more and more responsibility for my own emotional health. As I do this I affirm my child-within and rename her a survivor—no longer a victim.

❖ I am learning to enjoy my maturity and look forward to feeling the power of being responsible
for my own life.

I Can Stay Alive by Choosing to Live in the Moment

There may be many times in my life when my fear or self-loathing becomes so intense, that I feel I cannot go on. In the past I may have chosen to be hospitalized to keep me from harming myself or others. I need to commend myself for doing this. This action kept me and my precious spirit alive so that we could continue our healing process.

Today those same feelings may come back to me with the same intensity. However, because of my continuing recovery, I know that I have choices today other than hospitalization. I can allow that choice to be one of my last resorts and trust that I and other guides in my life will know when I need to utilize that option.

In the meantime I can stay alive by using my recovery tools and choose to live only in the moment. This means that I will not look nor think any further than what is occurring in the present moment in my life. I will focus on the present moment by noticing my surroundings, what I am seeing, what I am hearing, and how I am feeling. I may even choose to write this down to concretely affirm these facts for myself. This action will help to "ground" me in the reality of the present.

At times of less intensity, I may choose to look backward in order to feel feelings I have frozen. In this way I may heal and get on with my life. This is different from being overwhelmed by past feelings to the point of immobilization. Staying focused on the present moment can keep me safe, sane, alive, and functioning. I will use my creativity to choose activities to keep me focused on the present—like taking a walk, picking some flowers, washing the dishes, or running an errand. Whatever it takes, I will do.

✓ ❖   Today I am willing to do whatever it takes to remain in the present moment and to enjoy its fullness and beauty. This choice will help me to stay focused on the *reality* of the present moment in my life.

I Can Get Guidance in Learning to Parent My Child-Within

If I but look, I will notice many guides in my life. There are people who can help me learn to parent my child-within in a nurturing, kind way. I do not have to try to do this task alone. I will, in fact, need help in undoing some of the negative parenting skills I have internalized as a result of the abuse. I will need objective people who understand what children need to grow and flourish emotionally and spiritually.

I may find these guides in many places and at many different times in my life. Some will be a consistent part of my life, others I may know only for a fleeting moment. However I glean my parenting knowledge, my child-within will be that much richer and stronger in spirit.

Each time I actively employ some of the knowledge I am receiving from my guides, I will be demonstrating to my child-within my love for her and my compassion for her past abuses. She deserves to be parented in a loving, respectful way, and today I can begin to give that to her. There are many guides available and she will help me know just what she needs from each one.

❖ **I am beginning to learn what healthy parenting is all about. I can get help as I learn to parent my own precious child-within.**

I Am Learning to Be Gentle with Myself

One of the qualities that was not bestowed on me as a child was that of gentleness. The sexual abuse certainly was not gentle to my body, spirit, emotions, or intellect. Instead I received harshness, disrespect, and sometimes brutality. It is not surprising that one of the most difficult things for me to give myself today is gentleness.

Whenever I am feeling critical of myself, I will stop and remember that this criticism emanates from the messages I received from my abusers. Today, instead of continuing to support this false legacy, I will begin to replace this critical thought with one I originally deserved to hear—one of gentleness and support of my precious being. This is how I can continue to hold the appropriate people accountable and be-

gin to adopt a much deserved attitude of gentleness toward myself.

Above all else, in my process of recovery from sexual abuse, I need to be most gentle with *all* parts of myself. I have too long borne the burden of someone
else's disease and shame.

Today I can be most gentle with myself by honoring and respecting my feelings and affirming the
beautiful and unique pace of my own process. In times
of great pain and fear, I will treat myself as I would
a very young child—with understanding, patience,
and gentleness.

✦ **Just for today I will recognize and affirm one
way that I have been gentle with my healing-self.**

119

Helpful Resources

Books

Bass, Ellen and Laura Davis. *The Courage to Heal.* New York: Harper & Row, 1988.

Beattie, Melody. *Beyond CoDependence.* San Francisco: Harper & Row, 1989.

Berkus, Rusty. *To Heal Again.* Encino, CA: Red Rose Press, 1986.

Black, Claudia. *It's Never Too Late to Have a Happy Childhood.* New York: Ballantine Books, 1989.

Blume, E. Sue. *Secret Survivors.* New York: John Wiley and Sons, 1990.

Bozarth-Campbell, Alla. *Life Is Goodbye, Life Is Hello.* Minneapolis: Compcare, 1982.

Daugherty, Lynn B. *Why Me?* Racine, WI: Mother Courage Press, 1984.

Fahy, Mary. *The Tree That Survived the Winter.* Mahwah, NJ: Paulist Press, 1989.

Forward, Dr. Susan with Craig Buck. *Toxic Parents.* New York: Bantam Books, 1989.

Gil, Eliana. *Outgrowing the Pain.* New York: Dell, 1983.

Hartman, Cherry. *Be-Good-to-Yourself Therapy.* St. Munrad, IN: Abbey Press, 1987.

Love, Dr. Patricia. *The Emotional Incest Syndrome.* New York: Bantam Books, 1990.

Maltz, Wendy and Beverly Holman. *Incest and Sexuality.* Washington, D.C.: Lexington Books, 1987.

Mellody, Pia with Andrea Wells Miller and J. Keith Miller. *Facing Co-Dependence.* San Francisco: Harper & Row, 1989.

Middleton-Moz, Jane and Lorie Dwinell. *After the Tears.* Pompano Beach, FL: Health Communications, 1986.

Pamphlets

Caruso, Beverly. *The Impact of Incest.* Center City, MN: Hazelden, 1987.

Haury, Don. *I'm Not My Fault.* Scottsdale, AZ: Safe Place Publishing, 1988.

Kunzman, Kristin A. *Healing from Childhood Sexual Abuse.* Center City, MN: Hazelden, 1989.

Tapes

Baldwin, Martha. *Change of Heart.* Oklahoma City, OK: Rainbow Books, 1989.

Fisher, Amy. *Healing the Spiritual Wound.* San Diego, CA: Listen to Learn Tapes, Recovery Resources, 1988.

Mellody, Pia. *Co-Dependency Recovery, Spirituality, and Self-Care.* Wickenburg, AZ: Listen to Learn Tapes, Recovery Resources, 1988.

Mellody, Pia. *Permission to Be Precious.* Wickenburg, AZ: Listen to Learn Tapes, Recovery Resources, 1987.

My Personal Index

It may be helpful to write down feelings or associations that come to mind when reading a certain affirmation, or to note which affirmation was helpful to you in a certain situation. For example, the affirmations "I Deserve to Wear Clothes That Flatter the Shape of My Body" and "I Love My Body" may have comforted you on a day when you felt self-conscious. You may want to write this down so that the next time you are confronted with these feelings, you can refer back to the affirmation that was of help.

Topic/Situation   Page

_____   _____

_____   _____

_____   _____

_____   _____

_____   _____

Topic/Situation   **Page**

Topic/Situation   **Page**

_____

_____

_____

_____

_____

_____

_____

_____

_____

_____

_____

_____

_____

_____

_____

_____

_____

_____

_____

_____

_____

_____

_____

_____

_____

_____

_____

_____

_____

_____

_____

_____

_____

_____

_____

_____

_____

_____

Topic/Situation   **Page**

_____

_____

_____

_____

_____

_____

_____

_____

_____

_____

_____

_____

_____

_____

_____

_____

_____

_____

_____

Topic/Situation	Page

Notes